JURISDICTIONAL HISTORIES
FOR
OHIO'S EIGHTY-EIGHT
COUNTIES

1788-1985

W. Louis Phillips, C.G.

HERITAGE BOOKS
2012

HERITAGE BOOKS

AN IMPRINT OF HERITAGE BOOKS, INC.

Books, CDs, and more—Worldwide

For our listing of thousands of titles see our website
at
www.HeritageBooks.com

Published 2012 by
HERITAGE BOOKS, INC.
Publishing Division
100 Railroad Ave. #104
Westminster, Maryland 21157

International Standard Book Numbers
Paperbound: 978-0-917890-81-9
Clothbound: 978-0-7884-9386-7

JURISDICTIONAL HISTORIES

for

OHIO'S EIGHTY-EIGHT COUNTIES

In order to pursue genealogical and historical research in county records it is essential to know the jurisdictional history of the counties since this determines where one must look for the records. When Ohio became a state in 1803 there were only seventeen counties. Over the years those counties were reduced in size and new counties were created so that by 1888 there were eighty-eight. The often complex jurisdictional histories of these eighty-eight counties poses a significant challenge to the researcher. By using this guide, researchers will be able to quickly ascertain the needed information.

The standard reference for jurisdictional changes in Ohio has been Randolph C. Downes' Evolution of Ohio County Boundaries which was originally published in "Ohio Archaelogical and Historical Publications," Vol. XXXVI (1927). It was reprinted in book form by the Ohio Historical Society (1970), but is currently out of print. Unfortunately, numerous errors appear in the 1970 reprint. A table of corrections and additions to that book is presented at the conclusion of this introduction.

Dr. Downes' approach was to present the various legislative acts which created or changed county boundaries in Ohio. Numerous maps were also constructed to portray the county boundaries at specific times (1790, 1792, 1797, 1799, 1801, 1803, 1806, etc.) through 1888 at which time they "solidified." Although quite helpful, Dr. Downes' treatment leaves much to be desired as far as the ordinary researcher is concerned.

The following tables depicting the jurisdictional histories of Ohio's eighty-eight counties were compiled in order to present the necessary information in a much more concise and readily usable form. They give the jurisdictional history of each of the modern counties in chronological order for the period prior to statehood up to the present. Only the area currently bounded by each county was taken into consideration in determining which counties had held jurisdiction in the past and for what time period. Some counties, such as Adams, Belmont, Clermont, Hamilton, Ross, Trumbull, Warren and Washington, have relatively simple histories with their present-day territory having only been governed by one or several county governments over the years. Generally, counties which were formed a considerable time after statehood have more complicated backgrounds. Allen Co., for example, was organized in 1831. Its current land area was governed totally, or in part, by fifteen different counties during the period 1796-1848.

It should be noted that extant records may not be available for a particular county of interest. For instance, in the following tables under Auglaize Co. it states that Hamilton Co exercised jurisdiction over part of what is now Auglaize Co. from 1792 till 1803. There will probably be no helpful records, however, at Hamilton Co. that would be relevant to Auglaize Co. because of the fires and floods that have plagued the Hamilton Co. Courthouse at Cincinnati. Also, even if there had not been any such tragedies, there were probably very few individuals and little activity in the area that was to become Auglaize Co. during 1792-1803.

The phrase "unattached lands" which appears in the following tables means that no county was responsible for the area so designated. Such regions were short-lived and were the result of an area not yet being included within a jurisdiction, or from errors arising from the lack of understanding of the topographical features of the land that was being divided.

The earliest commencing date for jurisdictional coverage in this publication is 27 July 1788. This represents the date of erection and organization of Washington County which originally covered nearly all of the eastern half of modern-day Ohio. The old Northwest Territory counties of Knox (which was later reduced to Knox Co., Indiana) and Wayne (which was later reduced to Wayne Co., Michigan) should not be confused with the present Ohio counties of Knox (organized 1808) and Wayne (organized 1812). The old counties of Knox and Wayne were not the parent counties of the present-day Ohio counties bearing those names.

The termination date for the jurisdictional coverage in northwestern Ohio by old Wayne Co. is listed in this publication as 30 April/1 May 1803, primarily as a matter of convenience because that is when Franklin, Greene and Montgomery counties began exercising jurisdiction over territory that was formerly governed by old Wayne Co.

I would like to acknowledge Mr. Harold G. Miller of Milford, Ohio whose interest and keen insight into the complex problem of Ohio's changing boundaries has made this publication more accurate. This revised and expanded description of the jurisdictional histories
of Ohio's counties supersedes my previous writings on this subject [1, 2].

W. Louis Phillips, C.G.
January 1986

----

1. W. Louis Phillips. "The Jurisdictional Histories of Ohio's 88 Counties." The Report (Ohio Genealogical Society) 22(4): 187-192, 1982.
2. W. Louis Phillips. "Additions and Corrections." ibid 23(1): 15, 1982.

CORRECTIONS AND ADDITIONS

to

Evolution of Ohio County Boundaries
by Randolph C. Downes

The following list of corrections and additions should be kept in mind by anyone working with Dr. Downes' compilation:

p.18 - 3rd line from the bottom, "Muskingum [River]" should read Tuscarawas River. The wording of the original legislation was: "...between it [portage] and the Tuscarawas branch of the Muskingum [River]...."

p.21 - 4th line from the bottom, "Hamilton from Adams" should read Adams from Hamilton.

p.41 - 3rd line from the bottom, "Butler from Hamilton" should read Hamilton from Butler.

p.46 - 13th line from the bottom, "April 1, 1810" should read April 1, 1811.

p.50 - 14th line from the bottom, "May 1, 1812" should read May 1, 1811.

p.52 - 6th line from the bottom, "January 29, 1813" should read March 1, 1813.

p.65 - 11th line from the bottom, "March 1, 1817" should read March 1, 1818.

p.67 - 1820 map of Ohio, the Huron-Sandusky border line should have extended across the Sandusky Bay and over the Marble-head Peninsula.

p.68 - 9th line from the top, "April 1, 1819" should read April 1, 1820.

p.68 - 10th line from the bottom, "April 1, 1819" should read April 1, 1820.

p.105 - 5th line from the top, "March 1, 1848" should read February 24, 1848.

p.114 - under Allen County, "March 1, 1820" should read April, 1 1820.

p.118 - under Crawford County, "April 1, 1824" should read May 1, 1824.

p.119 - under Delaware County, the following date and event should be inserted between February 17, 1809 and April 1, 1820: April 1, 1815 - diminished by enlargement of Huron.

p.124 - under Highland County, "May 1, 1805" should read March 1, 1805.

p.125 - under Huron County, the following date and event should be inserted between March 16, 1838 and February 24, 1846: March 6, 1840 - part attached to Erie.

p.127 - under Lorain County, "December 26, 1822 - Erected and attached to Cuyahoga and Lorain" should read Cuyahoga and Medina.

p.127 - under Lorain County, "April 21, 1824" should read April 1, 1824.

p.128 - under Madison County, the following date and event should be inserted between April 1, 1820 and March 4, 1845: January 22, 1827 - boundary with Clark altered.

p.128 - under Marion County, "March 1, 1824" should read May 1, 1824.

p.130 - under Morgan County, the following date and event should be inserted between March 1, 1819 and March 11, 1845: December 24, 1819 - part attached to Monroe.

OHIO COUNTIES
AND
COUNTY SEATS

Present-Day Counties	Time Periods	Governing Counties
Adams Co.		
	July 27, 1788 - Feb. 11, 1792	unattached lands
	Feb. 11, 1792 - July 10, 1797	Hamilton
	July 10, 1797 - present	Adams

Allen Co.		
	Feb. 11, 1792 - Aug. 15, 1796	Hamilton & Knox (old)
	Aug. 15, 1796 - May 1, 1803	Wayne (old)
	May 1, 1803 - Mar. 1, 1805	Montgomery & Greene
	Mar. 1, 1805 - Jan. 7, 1812	Montgomery & Champaign
	Jan. 7, 1812 - Mar. 1, 1818	Miami & Champaign
	Mar. 1, 1818 - Apr. 1, 1819	Miami & Logan
	Apr. 1, 1819 - Apr. 1, 1820	Shelby & Logan
	Apr. 1, 1820 - Jan. 2, 1824	Shelby, Wood & Darke
	Jan. 2, 1824 - Feb. 2, 1824	Shelby, Wood & Mercer
	Feb. 2, 1824 - Mar. 1, 1828	Shelby, Williams & Mercer
	Mar. 1, 1828 - Mar. 1, 1831	Williams & Mercer
	Mar. 1, 1831 - Jan. 3, 1834	Allen, Williams & Mercer
	Jan. 3, 1834 - Mar. 18, 1837	Allen, Putnam & Mercer
	Mar. 18, 1837 - Feb. 14, 1848	Allen, Putnam, Mercer & Van Wert
	Feb. 14, 1848 - present	Allen

Ashland Co.		
	Aug. 15, 1796 - July 10, 1800	Wayne (old) & unattached lands
	July 10, 1800 - Apr. 30, 1803	Wayne (old), Trumbull & unattached lands
	Apr. 30, 1803 - Feb. 13, 1808	Trumbull & unattached lands
	Feb. 13, 1808 - Mar. 1, 1808	Trumbull, Columbiana & unattached lands
	Mar. 1, 1808 - June 7, 1808	Trumbull, Columbiana & Knox
	June 7, 1808 - Jan. 1, 1809	Portage, Columbiana & Knox

(cont. on next page)

Present-Day Counties	Time Periods	Governing Counties
Ashland Co. (cont.)		
	Jan. 1, 1809 - May 1, 1810	Portage, Stark & Knox
	May 1, 1810 - Mar. 1, 1812	Portage, Stark, Knox & Cuyahoga
	Mar. 1, 1812 - Mar. 1, 1813	Portage, Wayne, Knox & Cuyahoga
	Mar. 1, 1813 - Apr. 1, 1815	Portage, Wayne, Richland & Cuyahoga
	Apr. 1, 1815 - Jan. 14, 1818	Portage, Wayne, Richland & Huron
	Jan. 14, 1818 - Apr. 1, 1824	Medina, Wayne, Richland & Huron
	Apr. 1, 1824 - Feb. 24, 1846	Lorain, Wayne, Richland & Huron
	Feb. 24, 1846 - present	Ashland

Ashtabula Co.		
	July 27, 1788 - July 29, 1797	Washington
	July 29, 1797 - July 10, 1800	Jefferson
	July 10, 1800 - Mar. 1, 1806	Trumbull
	Mar. 1, 1806 - May 1, 1811	Trumbull & Geauga
	May 1, 1811 - present	Ashtabula

Athens Co.		
	July 27, 1788 - Mar. 1, 1805	Washington
	Mar. 1, 1805 - Feb. 10, 1814	Athens & Washington
	Feb. 10, 1814 - present	Athens

Auglaize Co.		
	Feb. 11, 1792 - Aug. 15, 1796	Hamilton & Knox (old)
	Aug. 15, 1796 - June 22, 1798	Wayne (old) & Knox (old)
	June 22, 1798 - May 1, 1803	Wayne (old) & Hamilton
	May 1, 1803 - Mar. 1, 1805	Montgomery & Greene
	Mar. 1, 1805 - Jan. 7, 1812	Montgomery & Champaign
	(cont. on next page)	

Present-Day Counties	Time Periods	Governing Counties
Auglaize Co. (cont.)		
	Jan. 7, 1812 - Mar. 1, 1817	Miami & Champaign
	Mar. 1, 1817 - Mar. 1, 1818	Miami, Champaign & Darke
	Mar. 1, 1818 - Apr. 1, 1819	Miami, Logan & Darke
	Apr. 1, 1819 - Jan. 2, 1824	Shelby & Darke
	Jan. 2, 1824 - Mar. 1, 1828	Shelby & Mercer
	Mar. 1, 1828 - Mar. 1, 1831	Mercer
	Mar. 1, 1831 - Feb. 14, 1848	Mercer & Allen
	Feb. 14, 1848 - present	Auglaize

note: Mar. 15, 1888 - Auglaize-Logan line altered; see Downes' Evolution of Ohio County Boundaries, p. 112.

Present-Day Counties	Time Periods	Governing Counties
Belmont Co.		
	July 27, 1788 - July 29, 1797	Washington
	July 29, 1797 - Sep. 7, 1801	Washington & Jefferson
	Sep. 7, 1801 - present	Belmont

Present-Day Counties	Time Periods	Governing Counties
Brown Co.		
	Feb. 11, 1792 - July 10, 1797	Hamilton
	July 10, 1797 - Dec. 6, 1800	Hamilton & Adams
	Dec. 6, 1800 - Mar. 1, 1818	Clermont & Adams
	Mar. 1, 1818 - present	Brown

Present-Day Counties	Time Periods	Governing Counties
Butler Co.		
	June 20, 1790 - June 22, 1798	Hamilton & Knox (old)
	June 22, 1798 - May 1, 1803	Hamilton
	May 1, 1803 - present	Butler

Present-Day Counties	Time Periods	Governing Counties
Carroll Co.		
	July 27, 1788 - July 29, 1797	Washington
	July 29, 1797 - May 1, 1803	Washington & Jefferson
	May 1, 1803 - Mar. 1, 1804	Washington, Jefferson & Columbiana

(cont. on next page)

Present-Day Counties	Time Periods	Governing Counties

Carroll Co. (cont.)

	Mar. 1, 1804 - Jan. 31, 1807	Jefferson, Columbiana & unattached lands
	Jan. 31, 1807 - Jan. 1, 1809	Jefferson & Columbiana
	Jan. 1, 1809 - Feb. 11, 1809	Jefferson, Columbiana & Stark
	Feb. 11, 1809 - Feb. 1, 1813	Jefferson, Columbiana, Stark & Tuscarawas
	Feb. 1, 1813 - Jan. 1, 1833	Jefferson, Columbiana, Stark Tuscarawas & Harrison
	Jan. 1, 1833 - present	Carroll

note: Feb. 3, 1834 - Carroll-Stark line altered; see Downes' Evolution of Ohio County Boundaries, pp.85-86.

Champaign Co.

	Feb. 11, 1792 - July 10, 1797	Hamilton
	July 10, 1797 - Aug. 20, 1798	Hamilton & Adams
	Aug. 20, 1798 - Apr. 30/May 1, 1803	Hamilton & Ross
	Apr. 30/May 1, 1803 - Mar. 1, 1805	Franklin & Greene
	Mar. 1, 1805 - present	Champaign

Clark Co.

	Feb. 11, 1792 - July 10, 1797	Hamilton
	July 10, 1797 - Aug. 20, 1798	Hamilton & Adams
	Aug. 20, 1798 - Apr. 30/May 1, 1803	Hamilton & Ross
	Apr. 30/May 1, 1803 - Mar. 1, 1805	Franklin & Greene
	Mar. 1, 1805 - Mar. 1, 1810	Franklin, Greene & Champaign
	Mar. 1, 1810 - Mar. 1, 1818	Madison, Greene & Champaign
	Mar. 1, 1818 - Feb. 25, 1819	Clark, Madison & Greene
	Feb. 25, 1819 - Jan. 22, 1827	Clark & Madison
	Jan. 22, 1827 - present	Clark

Present-Day Counties	Time Periods	Governing Counties

Clermont Co.

	July 27, 1788 - Feb. 11, 1792	unattached lands
	Feb. 11, 1792 - Dec. 6, 1800	Hamilton
	Dec. 6, 1800 - present	Clermont

Clinton Co.

	Feb. 11, 1792 - July 10, 1797	Hamilton
	July 10, 1797 - Aug. 20, 1798	Hamilton & Adams
	Aug. 20, 1798 - May 1, 1803	Hamilton & Ross
	May 1, 1803 - Mar. 1, 1805	Warren & Ross
	Mar. 1, 1805 - Mar. 1, 1810	Warren & Highland
	Mar. 1, 1810 - Mar. 1, 1815	Clinton, Warren & Highland
	Mar. 1, 1815 - present	Clinton

Columbiana Co.

	July 27, 1788 - July 29, 1797	Washington
	July 29, 1797 - May 1, 1803	Jefferson
	May 1, 1803 - present	Columbiana

Coshocton Co.

	July 27, 1788 - Dec. 9, 1800	Washington
	Dec. 9, 1800 - Mar. 1, 1804	Washington & Fairfield
	Mar. 1, 1804 - Mar. 15, 1808	Muskingum
	Mar. 15, 1808 - Apr. 1, 1811	Muskingum & Tuscarawas
	Apr. 1, 1811 - present	Coshocton

Crawford Co.

	Feb. 11, 1792 - Aug. 15, 1796	Hamilton & unattached lands
	Aug. 15, 1796 - Apr. 30, 1803	Wayne (old)
	Apr. 30, 1803 - Mar. 1, 1808	Franklin & unattached lands
	Mar. 1, 1808 - Feb. 17, 1809	Franklin & Knox
	Feb. 17, 1809 - Mar. 1, 1813	Delaware & Knox
	Mar. 1, 1813 - Feb. 17, 1824	Delaware & Richland
	Feb. 17, 1824 - May 1, 1824	Delaware, Richland & Seneca
	May 1, 1824 - Apr. 1, 1826	Marion, Richland & Seneca

(cont. on next page)

Present-Day Counties	Time Periods	Governing Counties
Crawford Co. (cont.)		
	Apr. 1, 1826 - Feb. 3, 1845	Crawford, Marion & Richland
	Feb. 3, 1845 - present	Crawford

Cuyahoga Co.		
	July 27, 1788 - Aug. 15, 1796	Washington & unattached lands
	Aug. 15, 1796 - July 29, 1797	Washington & Wayne (old)
	July 29, 1797 - July 10, 1800	Jefferson & Wayne (old)
	July 10, 1800 - Mar. 1, 1806	Trumbull
	Mar. 1, 1806 - June 7, 1808	Trumbull & Geauga
	June 7, 1808 - May 1, 1810	Geauga
	May 1, 1810 - Apr. 21, 1824	Cuyahoga & Geauga
	Apr. 21, 1824 - Jan. 29, 1827	Cuyahoga, Geauga & Lorain
	Jan. 29, 1827 - Jan. 11, 1843	Cuyahoga & Geauga
	Jan. 11, 1843 - present	Cuyahoga

Darke Co.		
	June 20, 1790 - June 22, 1798	Knox (old)
	June 22, 1798 - Feb. 3, 1801	Hamilton & Knox (old)
	Feb. 3, 1801 - Apr. 30, 1802	Hamilton & Clark (IN)
	Apr. 30, 1802 - May 1, 1803	Hamilton
	May 1, 1803 - Mar. 1, 1807	Montgomery
	Mar. 1, 1807 - Mar. 1, 1817	Miami
	Mar. 1, 1817 - present	Darke

Defiance Co.		
	June 20, 1790 - Feb. 11, 1792	Knox (old)
	Feb. 11, 1792 - Aug. 15, 1796	Knox (old) & Hamilton
	Aug. 15, 1796 - May 7, 1800	Wayne (old)
	May 7, 1800 - Apr. 30, 1802	Knox (old) & Wayne (old)
	Apr. 30, 1802 - May 1, 1803	Wayne (old)
	May 1, 1803 - Jan. 7, 1812	Montgomery

(cont. on next page)

Present-Day Counties	Time Periods	Governing Counties
Defiance Co. (cont.)		
	Jan. 7, 1812 - Mar. 1, 1817	Miami
	Mar. 1, 1817 - Apr. 1, 1819	Miami & Darke
	Apr. 1, 1819 - Apr. 1, 1820	Shelby & Darke
	Apr. 1, 1820 - Feb. 2, 1824	Wood
	Feb. 2, 1824 - Dec. 26, 1834	Williams
	Dec. 26, 1834 - Mar. 18, 1839	Williams & Henry
	Mar. 18, 1839 - Apr. 7, 1845	Williams, Henry & Paulding
	Apr. 7, 1845 - present	Defiance
Delaware Co.		
	July 27, 1788 - Feb. 11, 1792	Washington & unattached lands
	Feb. 11, 1792 - July 10, 1797	Washington & Hamilton
	July 10, 1797 - Aug. 20, 1798	Adams
	Aug. 20, 1798 - Dec. 9, 1800	Ross
	Dec. 9, 1800 - Apr. 30, 1803	Ross & Fairfield
	Apr. 30, 1803 - Mar. 1, 1808	Franklin & Fairfield
	Mar. 1, 1808 - Apr. 1, 1808	Franklin
	Apr. 1, 1808 - present	Delaware
Erie Co.		
	Aug. 15, 1796 - July 10, 1800	Wayne (old)
	July 10, 1800 - Mar. 1, 1806	Trumbull
	Mar. 1, 1806 - May 1, 1810	Geauga
	May 1, 1810 - Apr. 1, 1815	Cuyahoga
	Apr. 1, 1815 - Mar. 16, 1838	Huron
	Mar. 16, 1838 - Mar. 6, 1840	Erie & Huron
	Mar. 6, 1840 - present	Erie

Present-Day Counties	Time Periods	Governing Counties

Fairfield Co.

	July 27, 1788 - July 10, 1797	Washington
	July 10, 1797 - Aug. 20, 1798	Washington & Adams
	Aug. 20, 1798 - Dec. 9, 1800	Washington & Ross
	Dec. 9, 1800 - present	Fairfield

Fayette Co.

	Feb. 11, 1792 - July 10, 1797	Hamilton
	July 10, 1797 - Aug. 20, 1798	Adams
	Aug. 20, 1798 - May 1, 1805	Ross
	May 1, 1805 - Mar. 1, 1810	Ross & Highland
	Mar. 1, 1810 - present	Fayette

Franklin Co.

	July 27, 1788 - Feb. 11, 1792	Washington & unattached lands
	Feb. 11, 1792 - July 10, 1797	Washington & Hamilton
	July 10, 1797 - Aug. 20, 1798	Adams
	Aug. 20, 1798 - Dec. 9, 1800	Ross
	Dec. 9, 1800 - Apr. 30, 1803	Ross & Fairfield
	Apr. 30, 1803 - Mar. 1, 1808	Franklin & Fairfield
	Mar. 1, 1808 - Jan. 27, 1817	Franklin, Fairfield & Licking
	Jan. 27, 1817 - Mar. 25, 1851	Franklin & Fairfield
	Mar. 25, 1851 - present	Franklin

note: Mar. 14, 1845 - Franklin-Madison line altered; see Downes' Evolution of Ohio County Boundaries, pp.93-94.

Fulton Co.

	Feb. 11, 1792 - Aug. 15, 1796	Hamilton & Knox (old)
	Aug. 15, 1796 - May 1, 1803	Wayne (old)
	May 1, 1803 - Mar. 1, 1805	Montgomery & Greene
	Mar. 1, 1805 - Jan. 7, 1812	Montgomery & Champaign
	Jan. 7, 1812 - Mar. 1, 1818	Miami & Champaign
	Mar. 1, 1818 - Apr. 1, 1819	Miami & Logan

(cont. on next page)

Present-Day Counties	Time Periods	Governing Counties
Fulton Co. (cont.)		
	Apr. 1, 1819 - Apr. 1, 1820	Shelby & Logan
	Apr. 1, 1820 - Feb. 2, 1824	Wood
	Feb. 2, 1824 - Dec. 26, 1834	Williams
	Dec. 26, 1834 - June 20, 1835	Williams & Henry
	June 20, 1835 - Apr. 1, 1850	Williams, Henry & Lucas
	Apr. 1, 1850 - present	Fulton
Gallia Co.		
	July 27, 1788 - Apr. 30, 1803	Washington
	Apr. 30, 1803 - Mar. 1, 1817	Gallia
	Mar. 1, 1817 - Feb. 11, 1840	Gallia & Lawrence
	Feb. 11, 1840 - present	Gallia
Geauga Co.		
	July 27, 1788 - July 29, 1797	Washington
	July 29, 1797 - July 10, 1800	Jefferson
	July 10, 1800 - Mar. 1, 1806	Trumbull
	Mar. 1, 1806 - present	Geauga
Greene Co.		
	Jan. 2, 1790 - Feb. 11, 1792	Hamilton & unattached lands
	Feb. 11, 1792 - July 10, 1797	Hamilton
	July 10, 1797 - Aug. 20, 1798	Hamilton & Adams
	Aug. 20, 1798 - May 1, 1803	Hamilton & Ross
	May 1, 1803 - present	Greene
Guernsey Co.		
	July 27, 1788 - Sep. 7, 1801	Washington
	Sep. 7, 1801 - Mar. 1, 1804	Washington & Belmont
	Mar. 1, 1804 - Mar. 1, 1810	Muskingum & Belmont
	Mar. 1, 1810 - present	Guernsey

Present-Day Counties	Time Periods	Governing Counties
Hamilton Co.		
	Jan. 2, 1790 - June 20, 1790	Hamilton & unattached lands
	June 20, 1790 - Feb. 11, 1792	Hamilton, Knox (old) & unattached lands
	Feb. 11, 1792 - June 22, 1798	Hamilton & knox (old)
	June 22, 1798 - May 1, 1803	Hamilton
	May 1, 1803 - Jan. 20, 1808	Hamilton & Butler
	Jan. 20, 1808 - present	Hamilton

Hancock Co.		
	Feb. 11, 1792 - Aug. 15, 1796	Hamilton
	Aug. 15, 1796 - Apr. 30/May 1, 1803	Wayne (old)
	Apr. 30/May 1, 1803 - Mar. 1, 1805	Franklin & Greene
	Mar. 1, 1805 - Feb. 17, 1809	Franklin & Champaign
	Feb. 17, 1809 - Apr. 1, 1815	Delaware & Champaign
	Apr. 1, 1815 - Mar. 1, 1818	Huron & Champaign
	Mar. 1, 1818 - Apr. 1, 1820	Huron & Logan
	Apr. 1, 1820 - Mar. 1, 1828	Wood
	Mar. 1, 1828 - present	Hancock

Hardin Co.		
	Feb. 11, 1792 - Aug. 15, 1796	Hamilton
	Aug. 15, 1796 - Apr. 30/May 1, 1803	Wayne (old)
	Apr. 30/May 1, 1803 - Mar. 1, 1805	Franklin & Greene
	Mar. 1, 1805 - Feb. 17, 1809	Franklin & Champaign
	Feb. 17, 1809 - Mar. 1, 1818	Delaware & Champaign
	Mar. 1, 1818 - Apr. 1, 1820	Delaware & Logan
	Apr. 1, 1820 - Mar. 1, 1833	Logan
	Mar. 1, 1833 - present	Hardin

Present-Day Counties	Time Periods	Governing Counties
Harrison Co.		
	July 27, 1788 - July 29, 1797	Washington
	July 29, 1797 - Mar. 1, 1804	Washington & Jefferson
	Mar. 1, 1804 - July 31, 1807	Jefferson & unattached lands
	July 31, 1807 - Mar. 15, 1808	Jefferson
	Mar. 15, 1808 - Feb. 1, 1813	Jefferson & Tuscarawas
	Feb. 1, 1813 - Jan. 1, 1833	Harrison & Tuscarawas
	Jan. 1, 1833 - present	Harrison

Present-Day Counties	Time Periods	Governing Counties
Henry Co.		
	Feb. 11, 1792 - Aug. 15, 1796	Hamilton & Knox (old)
	Aug. 15, 1796 - May 1, 1803	Wayne (old)
	May 1, 1803 - Mar. 1, 1805	Montgomery & Greene
	Mar. 1, 1805 - Jan. 7, 1812	Montgomery & Champaign
	Jan. 7, 1812 - Mar. 1, 1818	Miami & Champaign
	Mar. 1, 1818 - Apr. 1, 1819	Miami & Logan
	Apr. 1, 1819 - Apr. 1, 1820	Shelby & Logan
	Apr. 1, 1820 - Feb. 2, 1824	Wood
	Feb. 2, 1824 - Dec. 26, 1834	Williams
	Dec. 26, 1834 - present	Henry

Present-Day Counties	Time Periods	Governing Counties
Highland Co.		
	Feb. 11, 1792 - July 10, 1797	Hamilton
	July 10, 1797 - Aug. 20, 1798	Hamilton & Adams
	Aug. 20, 1798 - Dec. 6, 1800	Hamilton, Adams & Ross
	Dec. 6, 1800 - Mar. 1, 1805	Clermont, Adams & Ross
	Mar. 1, 1805 - Mar. 1, 1818	Highland & Clermont
	Mar. 1, 1818 - Oct. 27, 1874	Highland & Brown
	Oct. 27, 1874 - present	Highland

Present-Day Counties	Time Periods	Governing Counties
Hocking Co.		
	July 27, 1788 - July 10, 1797	Washington
	July 10, 1797 - Aug. 20, 1798	Washington & Adams
	Aug. 20, 1798 - Dec. 9, 1800	Washington & Ross
	Dec. 9, 1800 - Mar. 1, 1805	Washington, Ross & Fairfield
	Mar. 1, 1805 - Mar. 1, 1818	Athens, Ross & Fairfield
	Mar. 1, 1818 - Mar. 23, 1850	Hocking, Athens & Fairfield
	Mar. 23, 1850 - present	Hocking

Present-Day Counties	Time Periods	Governing Counties
Holmes Co.		
	July 27, 1788 - Aug. 15, 1796	Washington & unattached lands
	Aug. 15, 1796 - Dec. 9, 1800	Washington, Wayne (old) & unattached lands
	Dec. 9, 1800 - Apr. 30, 1803	Washington, Wayne (old), Fairfield & unattached lands
	Apr. 30, 1803 - Mar. 1, 1804	Washington, Fairfield & unattached lands
	Mar. 1, 1804 - Feb. 13, 1808	Muskingum & unattached lands
	Feb. 13, 1808 - Mar. 15, 1808	Muskingum & Columbiana
	Mar. 15, 1808 - Jan. 1, 1809	Muskingum, Columbiana & Tuscarawas
	Jan. 1, 1809 - Apr. 1, 1811	Muskingum, Tuscarawas & Stark
	Apr. 1, 1811 - Mar. 1, 1812	Coshocton, Tuscarawas & Stark
	Mar. 1, 1812 - Jan. 4, 1825	Coshocton, Tuscarawas & Wayne
	Jan. 4, 1825 - present	Holmes

Present-Day Counties	Time Periods	Governing Counties
Huron Co.		
	Aug. 15, 1796 - July 10, 1800	Wayne (old)
	July 10, 1800 - June 7, 1808	Trumbull

(cont. on next page)

Present-Day Counties	Time Periods	Governing Counties
Huron Co. (cont.)		
	June 7, 1808 - May 1, 1810	Portage
	May 1, 1810 - Apr. 1, 1815	Cuyahoga
	Apr. 1, 1815 - present	Huron
Jackson Co.		
	July 27, 1788 - July 10, 1797	Washington
	July 10, 1797 - Aug. 20, 1798	Washington & Adams
	Aug. 20, 1798 - Apr. 30, 1803	Washington, Adams & Ross
	Apr. 30, 1803 - May 1, 1803	Gallia, Adams & Ross
	May 1, 1803 - Mar. 1, 1816	Gallia, Scioto & Ross
	Mar. 1, 1816 - Mar. 1, 1818	Jackson, Gallia, Pike & Ross
	Mar. 1, 1818 - Feb. 7, 1843	Jackson, Gallia & Pike
	Feb. 7, 1843 - Mar. 23, 1850	Jackson & Gallia
	Mar. 23, 1850 - present	Jackson
Jefferson Co.		
	July 27, 1788 - July 29, 1797	Washington
	July 29, 1797 - May 1, 1803	Jefferson
	May 1, 1803 - Jan. 1, 1833	Jefferson & Columbiana
	Jan. 1, 1833 - present	Jefferson
Knox Co.		
	July 27, 1788 - July 10, 1797	Washington
	July 10, 1797 - Aug. 20, 1798	Washington & Adams
	Aug. 20, 1798 - Dec. 9, 1800	Washington & Ross
	Dec. 9, 1800 - Apr. 30, 1803	Fairfield, Ross & unattached lands
	Apr. 30, 1803 - Mar. 1, 1808	Fairfield & unattached lands
	Mar. 1, 1808 - present	Knox

Present-Day Counties	Time Periods	Governing Counties

Lake Co.

	Time Periods	Governing Counties
	July 27, 1788 - July 29, 1797	Washington
	July 29, 1797 - July 10, 1800	Jefferson
	July 10, 1800 - Mar. 1, 1806	Trumbull
	Mar. 1, 1806 - May 1, 1810	Geauga
	May 1, 1810 - Mar. 20, 1840	Geauga & Cuyahoga
	Mar. 20, 1840 - present	Lake

Lawrence Co.

	Time Periods	Governing Counties
	July 27, 1788 - July 10, 1797	Washington
	July 10, 1797 - Apr. 30, 1803	Washington & Adams
	Apr. 30, 1803 - May 1, 1803	Gallia & Adams
	May 1, 1803 - Mar. 1, 1817	Gallia & Scioto
	Mar. 1, 1817 - Feb. 11, 1840	Lawrence & Gallia
	Feb. 11, 1840 - present	Lawrence

Licking Co.

	Time Periods	Governing Counties
	July 27, 1788 - July 10, 1797	Washington
	July 10, 1797 - Aug. 20, 1798	Washington & Adams
	Aug. 20, 1798 - Dec. 9, 1800	Washington & Ross
	Dec. 9, 1800 - Mar. 1, 1808	Fairfield
	Mar. 1, 1808 - present	Licking

Logan Co.

	Time Periods	Governing Counties
	Feb. 11, 1792 - Aug. 15, 1796	Hamilton
	Aug. 15, 1796 - July 10, 1797	Hamilton & Wayne (old)
	July 10, 1797 - Aug. 20, 1798	Hamilton, Wayne (old) & Adams
	Aug. 20, 1798 - Apr. 30/May 1, 1803	Hamilton, Wayne (old) & Ross
	Apr. 30/May 1, 1803 - Mar. 1, 1805	Franklin & Greene
	Mar. 1, 1805 - Mar. 1, 1818	Champaign
	Mar. 1, 1818 - present	Logan

note: Apr. 11, 1883 - Logan-Shelby line altered; see
Downes' Evolution of Ohio County Boundaries, pp.111-112.

(cont. on next page)

```
Present-Day
Counties          Time Periods            Governing Counties
```

Logan Co. (cont.)

  note: Mar. 15, 1888 - Logan-Auglaize line altered; see
        Downes' Evolution of Ohio County Boundaries, pp.112-113.

Lorain Co.

Aug. 15, 1796 - July 10, 1800	Wayne (old)
July 10, 1800 - June 7, 1808	Trumbull
June 7, 1808 - May 1, 1810	Geauga & Portage
May 1, 1810 - Apr. 1, 1815	Cuyahoga & Portage
Apr. 1, 1815 - Jan. 14, 1818	Cuyahoga, Portage & Huron
Jan. 14, 1818 - Apr. 1, 1824	Cuyahoga, Medina & Huron
Apr. 1, 1824 - Jan. 29, 1827	Lorain & Medina
Jan. 29, 1827 - present	Lorain

Lucas Co.

Feb. 11, 1792 - Aug. 15, 1796	Hamilton
Aug. 15, 1796 - Apr. 30/May 1, 1803	Wayne (old)
Apr. 30/May 1, 1803 - Mar. 1, 1805	Franklin & Greene
Mar. 1, 1805 - Apr. 1, 1808	Franklin & Champaign
Apr. 1, 1808 - Apr. 1, 1815	Delaware & Champaign
Apr. 1, 1815 - Mar. 1, 1818	Huron & Champaign
Mar. 1, 1818 - Apr. 1, 1820	Huron & Logan
Apr. 1, 1820 - June 20, 1835	Sandusky & Wood
June 20, 1835 - Mar. 14, 1836	Lucas & Wood
Mar. 14, 1836 - Mar. 6, 1840	Lucas
Mar. 6, 1840 - Apr. 1, 1850	Lucas & Ottawa
Apr. 1, 1850 - present	Lucas

Madison Co.

Feb. 11, 1792 - July 10, 1797	Hamilton
July 10, 1797 - Aug. 20, 1798	Adams
Aug. 20, 1798 - Apr. 30, 1803	Ross

(cont. on next page)

Present-Day Counties	Time Periods	Governing Counties
Madison Co. (cont.)		
	Apr. 30, 1803 - Mar. 1, 1805	Franklin
	Mar. 1, 1805 - Mar. 1, 1810	Franklin & Champaign
	Mar. 1, 1810 - Mar. 1, 1818	Madison, Franklin & Champaign
	Mar. 1, 1818 - Jan. 22, 1827	Madison, Franklin & Clark
	Jan. 22, 1827 - Mar. 4, 1845	Madison & Franklin
	Mar. 4, 1845 - present	Madison
Mahoning Co.		
	July 27, 1788 - July 29, 1797	Washington
	July 29, 1797 - July 10, 1800	Jefferson
	July 10, 1800 - May 1, 1803	Jefferson & Trumbull
	May 1, 1803 - Mar. 1, 1846	Columbiana & Trumbull
	Mar. 1, 1846 - present	Mahoning
Marion Co.		
	Feb. 11, 1792 - Aug. 15, 1796	Hamilton & unattached lands
	Aug. 15, 1796 - July 10, 1797	Hamilton & Wayne (old)
	July 10, 1797 - Aug. 20, 1798	Wayne (old) & Adams
	Aug. 20, 1798 - Apr. 30, 1803	Wayne (old) & Ross
	Apr. 30, 1803 - Apr. 1, 1808	Franklin
	Apr. 1, 1808 - Feb. 17, 1809	Franklin & Delaware
	Feb. 17, 1809 - May 1, 1824	Delaware
	May 1, 1824 - Mar. 1, 1848	Marion & Delaware
	Mar. 1, 1848 - present	Marion
Medina Co.		
	Aug. 15, 1796 - July 10, 1800	Wayne (old)
	July 10, 1800 - June 7, 1808	Trumbull
	June 7, 1808 - Jan. 14, 1818	Portage
	Jan. 14, 1818 - Jan. 29, 1827	Medina

(cont. on next page)

Present-Day Counties	Time Periods	Governing Counties

Medina Co. (cont.)

	Jan. 29, 1827 - Mar. 3, 1840	Medina & Lorain
	Mar. 3, 1840 - present	Medina

note: Jan. 29, 1827 - Medina-Portage line altered; see Downes' Evolution of Ohio County Boundaries, pp.79-80.

Meigs Co.

	July 27, 1788 - Apr. 30, 1803	Washington
	Apr. 30, 1803 - Mar. 1, 1805	Washington & Gallia
	Mar. 1, 1805 - Apr. 1, 1819	Athens & Gallia
	Apr. 1, 1819 - present	Meigs

Mercer Co.

	June 20, 1790 - Aug. 15, 1796	Knox (old)
	Aug. 15, 1796 - June 22, 1798	Knox (old) & Wayne (old)
	June 22, 1798 - Feb. 3, 1801	Knox (old), Wayne (old) & Hamilton
	Feb. 3, 1801 - Apr. 30, 1802	Knox (old), Wayne (old), Hamilton & Clark (IN)
	Apr. 30, 1802 - May 1, 1803	Wayne (old) & Hamilton
	May 1, 1803 - Mar. 1, 1807	Montgomery
	Mar. 1, 1807 - Jan. 7, 1812	Montgomery & Miami
	Jan. 7, 1812 - Mar. 1, 1817	Miami
	Mar. 1, 1817 - Jan. 2, 1824	Darke
	Jan. 2, 1824 - Feb. 14, 1848	Mercer & Darke
	Feb. 14, 1848 - present	Mercer

Miami Co.

	June 20, 1790 - June 22, 1798	Hamilton & Knox (old)
	June 22, 1798 - May 1, 1803	Hamilton
	May 1, 1803 - Mar. 1, 1807	Montgomery
	Mar. 1, 1807 - present	Miami

Present-Day Counties	Time Periods	Governing Counties
Monroe Co.		
	July 27, 1788 - Sep. 7, 1801	Washington
	Sep. 7, 1801 - Mar. 1, 1810	Washington & Belmont
	Mar. 1, 1810 - Mar. 1, 1815	Washington, Belmont & Guernsey
	Mar. 1, 1815 - Apr. 1, 1851	Monroe & Washington
	Apr. 1, 1851 - present	Monroe

Montgomery Co.		
	June 20, 1790 - June 22, 1798	Hamilton & Knox (old)
	June 22, 1798 - May 1, 1803	Hamilton
	May 1, 1803 - present	Montgomery

Morgan Co.		
	July 27, 1788 - Mar. 1, 1804	Washington
	Mar. 1, 1804 - Mar. 1, 1805	Washington & Muskingum
	Mar. 1, 1805 - Mar. 1, 1810	Washington, Muskingum & Athens
	Mar. 1, 1810 - Mar. 1, 1819	Washington, Muskingum, Athens & Guernsey
	Mar. 1, 1819 - Mar. 11, 1845	Morgan, Washington & Athens
	Mar. 11, 1845 - Apr. 1, 1851	Morgan & Washington
	Apr. 1, 1851 - present	Morgan

Morrow Co.		
	Feb. 11, 1792 - Aug. 15, 1796	Hamilton, Washington & unattached lands
	Aug. 15, 1796 - July 10, 1797	Hamilton, Washington & Wayne (old)
	July 10, 1797 - Aug. 20, 1798	Adams & Wayne (old)
	Aug. 20, 1798 - Dec. 9, 1800	Ross & Wayne (old)
	Dec. 9, 1800 - Apr. 30, 1803	Ross, Fairfield & Wayne (old)
	Apr. 30, 1803 - Mar. 1, 1808	Franklin, Fairfield & unattached lands

(cont. on next page)

Present-Day Counties	Time Periods	Governing Counties

Morrow Co. (cont.)

	Mar. 1, 1808 - Feb. 17, 1809	Franklin, Delaware & knox
	Feb. 17, 1809 - Mar. 1, 1813	Delaware & Knox
	Mar. 1, 1813 - Mar. 1, 1824	Delaware, Knox & Richland
	Mar. 1, 1824 - Mar. 1, 1848	Delaware, Knox, Richland & Marion
	Mar. 1, 1848 - present	Morrow

Muskingum Co.

	July 27, 1788 - Dec. 9, 1800	Washington
	Dec. 9, 1800 - Mar. 1, 1804	Washington & Fairfield
	Mar. 1, 1804 - present	Muskingum

Noble Co.

	July 27, 1788 - Sep. 7, 1801	Washington
	Sep. 7, 1801 - Mar. 1, 1804	Washington & Belmont
	Mar. 1, 1804 - Mar. 1, 1810	Washington, Belmont & Muskingum
	Mar. 1, 1810 - Mar. 1, 1815	Washington & Guernsey
	Mar. 1, 1815 - Mar. 1, 1819	Washington, Guernsey & Monroe
	Mar. 1, 1819 - Apr. 1, 1851	Washington, Guernsey, Monroe & Morgan
	Apr. 1, 1851 - present	Noble

Ottawa Co.

	Feb. 11, 1792 - Aug. 15, 1796	Hamilton & unattached lands
	Aug. 15, 1796 - July 10, 1800	Wayne (old)
	July 10, 1800 - Apr. 30, 1803	Wayne (old) & Trumbull
	Apr. 30, 1803 - Mar. 1, 1806	Franklin & Trumbull
	Mar. 1, 1806 - Feb. 17, 1809	Franklin & Geauga
	Feb. 17, 1809 - May 1, 1810	Delaware & Geauga
	May 1, 1810 - Apr. 1, 1815	Delaware & Cuyahoga

(cont. on next page)

Present-Day Counties	Time Periods	Governing Counties
Ottawa Co. (cont.)		
	Apr. 1, 1815 - Apr. 1, 1820	Huron
	Apr. 1, 1820 - Mar. 16, 1838	Huron & Sandusky
	Mar. 16, 1838 - Mar. 6, 1840	Erie & Sandusky
	Mar. 6, 1840 - present	Ottawa

Paulding Co.		
	June 20, 1790 - Aug. 15, 1796	Knox (old)
	Aug. 15, 1796 - May 7, 1800	Wayne (old)
	May 7, 1800 - Apr. 30, 1802	Wayne (old) & Knox (old)
	Apr. 30, 1802 - May 1, 1803	Wayne (old)
	May 1, 1803 - Jan. 7, 1812	Montgomery
	Jan. 7, 1812 - Mar. 1, 1817	Miami
	Mar. 1, 1817 - Apr. 1, 1819	Miami & Darke
	Apr. 1, 1819 - Apr. 1, 1820	Shelby & Darke
	Apr. 1, 1820 - Feb. 2, 1824	Wood
	Feb. 2, 1824 - Mar. 18, 1839	Williams
	Mar. 18, 1839 - present	Paulding

Perry Co.		
	July 27, 1788 - Dec. 9, 1800	Washington
	Dec. 9, 1800 - Mar. 1, 1804	Washington & Fairfield
	Mar. 1, 1804 - Mar. 1, 1818	Washington, Fairfield & Muskingum
	Mar. 1, 1818 - Feb. 20, 1837	Perry & Licking
	Feb. 20, 1837 - present	Perry

Pickaway Co.		
	July 27, 1788 - Feb. 11, 1792	Washington & unattached lands
	Feb. 11, 1792 - July 10, 1797	Washington & Hamilton

(cont. on next page)

Present-Day Counties	Time Periods	Governing Counties
Pickaway Co. (cont.)		
	July 10, 1797 - Apr. 20, 1798	Adams
	Apr. 20, 1798 - Dec. 9, 1800	Ross
	Dec. 9, 1800 - Apr. 30, 1803	Ross & Fairfield
	Apr. 30, 1803 - Mar. 1, 1810	Ross, Fairfield & Franklin
	Mar. 1, 1810 - present	Pickaway

Pike Co.

	Jan. 27, 1788 - Feb. 11, 1792	Washington & unattached lands
	Feb. 11, 1792 - July 10, 1797	Washington & Hamilton
	July 10, 1797 - Aug. 20, 1798	Adams
	Aug. 20, 1798 - May 1, 1803	Adams & Ross
	May 1, 1803 - Feb. 1, 1815	Adams, Ross & Scioto
	Feb. 1, 1815 - Mar. 1, 1816	Pike & Scioto
	Mar. 1, 1816 - Feb. 7, 1843	Pike & Jackson
	Feb. 7, 1843 - present	Pike

Portage Co.

	July 27, 1788 - July 29, 1797	Washington
	July 29, 1797 - July 10, 1800	Jefferson
	July 10, 1800 - June 7, 1808	Trumbull
	June 7, 1808 - present	Portage

note: Jan. 29, 1827 - Portage-Medina line altered; see Downes' _Evolution of Ohio County Boundaries_, pp. 79-80.

Preble Co.

	June 20, 1790 - June 22, 1798	Knox (old)
	June 22, 1798 - May 1, 1803	Hamilton
	May 1, 1803 - Mar. 1, 1808	Montgomery & Butler
	Mar. 1, 1808 - present	Preble

Present-Day Counties	Time Periods	Governing Counties

Putnam Co.

	Feb. 11, 1792 - Aug. 15, 1796	Hamilton & Knox (old)
	Aug. 15, 1796 - May 1, 1803	Wayne (old)
	May 1, 1803 - Mar. 1, 1805	Montgomery & Greene
	Mar. 1, 1805 - Jan. 7, 1812	Montgomery & Champaign
	Jan. 7, 1812 - Mar. 1, 1818	Miami & Champaign
	Mar. 1, 1818 - Apr. 1, 1819	Miami & Logan
	Apr. 1, 1819 - Apr. 1, 1820	Shelby & Logan
	Apr. 1, 1820 - Jan. 2, 1824	Wood & Darke
	Jan. 2, 1824 - Feb. 2, 1824	Wood & Mercer
	Feb. 2, 1824 - Jan. 3, 1834	Williams & Mercer
	Jan. 3, 1834 - Mar. 18, 1837	Putnam & Mercer
	Mar. 18, 1837 - Feb. 14, 1848	Putnam & Van Wert
	Feb. 14, 1848 - present	Putnam

Richland Co.

	Aug. 15, 1796 - July 10, 1797	Wayne (old)
	July 10, 1797 - Aug. 20, 1798	Wayne (old) & Adams
	Aug. 20, 1798 - Apr. 30, 1803	Wayne (old) & Ross
	Apr. 30, 1803 - Mar. 1, 1808	unattached lands
	Mar. 1, 1808 - Mar. 1, 1813	Knox
	Mar. 1, 1813 - Feb. 24, 1846	Richland
	Feb. 24, 1846 - Feb. 5, 1847	Richland & Ashland
	Feb. 5, 1847 - Feb. 24, 1848	Richland
	Feb. 24, 1848 - Mar. 22, 1849	Richland & Morrow
	Mar. 22, 1849 - present	Richland

Ross Co.

	July 27, 1788 - Feb. 11, 1792	Washington & unattached lands
	Feb. 11, 1792 - July 10, 1797	Washington & Hamilton

(cont. on next page)

Present-Day Counties	Time Periods	Governing Counties

Ross Co. (cont.)

	July 10, 1797 - Aug. 20, 1798	Adams
	Aug. 20, 1798 - present	Ross

note: Jan. 11, 1839 - Ross-Jackson line altered; see
    Downes' Evolution of Ohio County Boundaries, p. 87.

note: Mar. 7, 1843 - Ross-Pickaway line altered; see ibid.

Sandusky Co.

	Feb. 11, 1792 - Aug. 15, 1796	Hamilton & unattached lands
	Aug. 15, 1796 - Apr. 30, 1803	Wayne (old)
	Apr. 30, 1803 - Feb. 17, 1809	Franklin
	Feb. 17, 1809 - Apr. 1, 1815	Delaware
	Apr. 1, 1815 - Apr. 1, 1820	Huron
	Apr. 1, 1820 - Mar. 6, 1840	Sandusky
	Mar. 6, 1840 - Mar. 23, 1840	Sandusky & Ottawa
	Mar. 23, 1840 - present	Sandusky

Scioto Co.

	July 27, 1788 - Feb. 11, 1792	Washington & unattached lands
	Feb. 11, 1792 - July 10, 1797	Washington & Hamilton
	July 10, 1797 - May 1, 1803	Adams
	May 1, 1803 - Dec. 29, 1804	Scioto & Gallia
	Dec. 29, 1804 - Mar. 1, 1817	Scioto
	Mar. 1, 1817 - Mar. 1, 1826	Scioto & Lawrence
	Mar. 1, 1826 - present	Scioto

Seneca Co.

	Feb. 11, 1792 - Aug. 15, 1796	Hamilton & unattached lands
	Aug. 15, 1796 - Apr. 30, 1803	Wayne (old)
	Apr. 30, 1803 - Feb. 17, 1809	Franklin
	Feb. 17, 1809 - Apr. 1, 1815	Delaware
	Apr. 1, 1815 - Apr. 1, 1820	Huron
	Apr. 1, 1820 - Apr. 1, 1824	Sandusky
	Apr. 1, 1824 - present	Seneca

Present-Day Counties	Time Periods	Governing Counties
Shelby Co.		
	Feb. 11, 1792 - Aug. 15, 1796	Hamilton & Knox (old)
	Aug. 15, 1796 - June 22, 1798	Hamilton, Knox (old) & Wayne (old)
	June 22, 1798 - May 1, 1803	Hamilton & Wayne (old)
	May 1, 1803 - Mar. 1, 1807	Montgomery
	Mar. 1, 1807 - Jan. 7, 1812	Montgomery & Miami
	Jan. 7, 1812 - Apr. 1, 1819	Miami
	Apr. 1, 1819 - present	Shelby

note: Apr. 11, 1883 - Shelby-Logan line altered; see Downes' Evolution of Ohio County Boundaires, pp. 111-112.

Stark Co.		
	July 27, 1788 - Aug. 15, 1796	Washington & unattached lands
	Aug. 15, 1796 - Dec. 19, 1799	Washington, Wayne (old) & unattached lands
	Dec. 19, 1799 - May 1, 1803	Washington, Wayne (old), Jefferson & unattached lands
	May 1, 1803 - Feb. 13, 1808	Columbiana & unattached lands
	Feb. 13, 1808 - Jan. 1, 1809	Columbiana
	Jan. 1, 1809 - present	Stark

note: Feb. 3, 1834 - Stark-Carroll line altered; see Downes' Evolution of Ohio County Boundaries, pp. 85-86.

Summit Co.		
	July 27, 1788 - Aug. 15, 1796	Washington & unattached lands
	Aug. 15, 1796 - July 29, 1797	Washington & Wayne (old)
	July 29, 1797 - July 10, 1800	Washington, Wayne (old) & Jefferson
	July 10, 1800 - May 1, 1803	Washington, Wayne (old) & Trumbull
	May 1, 1803 - June 7, 1808	Trumbull, Columbiana & unattached lands

(cont. on next page)

Present-Day Counties	Time Periods	Governing Counties
Summit Co. (cont.)		
	June 7, 1808 - Jan. 1, 1809	Portage & Columbiana
	Jan. 1, 1809 - Jan. 14, 1818	Portage & Stark
	Jan. 14, 1818 - Mar. 17, 1840	Portage, Stark & Medina
	Mar. 17, 1840 - present	Summit

Trumbull Co.		
	July 27, 1788 - July 29, 1797	Washington
	July 29, 1797 - July 10, 1800	Jefferson
	July 10, 1800 - present	Trumbull

Tuscarawas Co.		
	July 27, 1788 - Mar. 1, 1804	Washington
	Mar. 1, 1804 - Jan. 31, 1807	Muskingum & unattached lands
	Jan. 31, 1807 - Mar. 15, 1808	Muskingum & Jefferson
	Mar. 15, 1808 - Feb. 11, 1809	Tuscarawas & Jefferson
	Feb. 11, 1809 - Feb. 4, 1848	Tuscarawas & Stark
	Feb. 4, 1848 - present	Tuscarawas

Union Co.		
	Feb. 11, 1792 - Aug. 15, 1796	Hamilton
	Aug. 15, 1796 - July 10, 1797	Hamilton & Wayne (old)
	July 10, 1797 - Aug. 20, 1798	Wayne (old) & Adams
	Aug. 20, 1798 - Apr. 30, 1803	Wayne (old) & Ross
	Apr. 30, 1803 - Mar. 1, 1805	Franklin
	Mar. 1, 1805 - Apr. 1, 1808	Franklin & Champaign
	Apr. 1, 1808 - Mar. 1, 1810	Franklin, Champaign & Delaware
	Mar. 1, 1810 - Mar. 1, 1818	Franklin, Champaign, Delaware & Madison
	Mar. 1, 1818 - Apr. 1, 1820	Franklin, Logan, Delaware & Madison
	Apr. 1, 1820 - present	Union

Present-Day Counties	Time Periods	Governing Counties
Van Wert Co.		
	June 20, 1790 - Aug. 15, 1796	Knox (old)
	Aug. 15, 1796 - June 22, 1798	Knox (old) & Wayne (old)
	June 22, 1798 - Apr. 30, 1802	Knox (old), Wayne (old) & Hamilton
	Apr. 30, 1802 - May 1, 1803	Wayne (old) & Hamilton
	May 1, 1803 - Jan. 7, 1812	Montgomery
	Jan. 7, 1812 - Mar. 1, 1817	Miami
	Mar. 1, 1817 - Apr. 1, 1819	Miami & Darke
	Apr. 1, 1819 - Apr. 1, 1820	Shelby & Darke
	Apr. 1, 1820 - Jan. 2, 1824	Darke
	Jan. 2, 1824 - Mar. 18, 1837	Mercer
	Mar. 18, 1837 - Feb. 14, 1848	Van Wert & Mercer
	Feb. 14, 1848 - present	Van Wert

Present-Day Counties	Time Periods	Governing Counties
Vinton Co.		
	July 27, 1788 - Aug. 20, 1798	Washington
	Aug. 20, 1798 - Apr. 30, 1803	Washington & Ross
	Apr. 30, 1803 - Mar. 1, 1805	Washington, Ross & Gallia
	Mar. 1, 1805 - Mar. 1, 1816	Athens, Ross & Gallia
	Mar. 1, 1816 - Mar. 1, 1818	Athens, Ross, Gallia & Jackson
	Mar. 1, 1818 - Mar. 23, 1850	Athens, Hocking, Gallia & Jackson
	Mar. 23, 1850 - present	Vinton

Present-Day Counties	Time Periods	Governing Counties
Warren Co.		
	June 20, 1790 - Feb. 11, 1792	Hamilton, Knox (old) & unattached lands
	Feb. 11, 1792 - June 22, 1798	Hamilton & Knox (old)
	June 22, 1798 - May 1, 1803	Hamilton
	May 1, 1803 - Mar. 1, 1815	Warren & Butler
	Mar. 1, 1815 - present	Warren

Present-Day Counties	Time Periods	Governing Counties
Washington Co.		
	July 27, 1788 - Mar. 1, 1805	Washington
	Mar. 1, 1805 - Feb. 10, 1814	Washington & Athens
	Feb. 10, 1814 - present	Washington

Wayne Co.		
	Aug. 15, 1796 - Apr. 30, 1803	Wayne (old)
	Apr. 30, 1803 - Feb. 13, 1808	unattached lands
	Feb.13, 1808 - Jan. 1, 1809	Columbiana
	Jan. 1, 1809 - Mar. 1, 1812	Stark
	Mar. 1, 1812 - present	Wayne

Williams Co.		
	June 20, 1790 - Aug. 15, 1796	Knox (old)
	Aug. 15, 1796 - May 7, 1800	Wayne (old)
	May 7, 1800 - Apr. 30, 1802	Wayne (old) & Knox (old)
	Apr. 30, 1802 - May 1, 1803	Wayne (old)
	May 1, 1803 - Jan. 7, 1812	Montgomery
	Jan. 7, 1812 - Mar. 1, 1817	Miami
	Mar. 1, 1817 - Apr. 1, 1819	Miami & Darke
	Apr. 1, 1819 - Apr. 1, 1820	Shelby & Darke
	Apr. 1, 1820 - Feb. 2, 1824	Wood
	Feb. 2, 1824 - present	Williams

Wood Co.		
	Feb. 11, 1792 - Aug. 15, 1796	Hamilton
	Aug. 15, 1796 - Apr. 30/May 1, 1803	Wayne (old)
	Apr. 30/May 1, 1803 - Mar. 1, 1805	Franklin & Greene
	Mar. 1, 1805 - Feb. 17, 1809	Franklin & Champaign
	Feb. 17, 1809 - Apr. 1, 1815	Delaware & Champaign
	Apr. 1, 1815 - Mar. 1, 1818	Huron & Champaign
	Mar. 1, 1818 - Apr. 1, 1820	Huron & Logan
	Apr. 1, 1820 - present	Wood

Present-Day Counties	Time Periods	Governing Counties
Wyandot Co.		
	Feb. 11, 1792 - Aug. 15, 1796	Hamilton
	Aug. 15, 1796 - Apr. 30, 1803	Wayne (old)
	Apr. 30, 1803 - Mar. 1, 1805	Franklin
	Mar. 1, 1805 - Feb. 17, 1809	Franklin & Champaign
	Feb. 17, 1809 - Mar. 1, 1818	Delaware & Champaign
	Mar. 1, 1818 - Apr. 1, 1820	Delaware & Logan
	Apr. 1, 1820 - Feb. 17, 1824	Delaware, Logan & Wood
	Feb. 17, 1824 - Apr. 1, 1824	Delaware, Logan, Wood & Sandusky
	Apr. 1, 1824 - May 1, 1824	Delaware, Logan, Wood & Seneca
	May 1, 1824 - Apr. 1, 1826	Marion, Logan, Wood & Seneca
	Apr. 1, 1826 - Mar. 1, 1828	Marion, Logan, Wood & Crawford
	Mar. 1, 1828 - Mar. 1, 1833	Marion, Logan, Hancock & Crawford
	Mar. 1, 1833 - Feb. 3, 1845	Marion, Hardin, Hancock & Crawford
	Feb. 3, 1845 - present	Wyandot

---

www.ingramcontent.com/pod-product-compliance
Lightning Source LLC
Chambersburg PA
CBHW081640040426

42449CB00014B/3391